NATURE NICK'S
ANIMAL ADVENTURES

NATURE NICK

To my mentor, Marc Morrone

CONTENTS

Preface:

You're Crazy If You Work with Kids AND Animals

If I wanted to work with animals, why didn't I just become a veterinarian? This is a common question that I am typically asked. Well it is harder to become a veterinarian than it is a medical doctor. If you don't believe me, ask someone who is applying to veterinary school as they often use medical school as their back up! A veterinary degree is one of the most expensive degrees one can pursue. You must also be good at mathematics and science, which are subjects I always did poorly in. In addition, many veterinarians only work with dogs and cats and are never exposed to exotic wildlife.

Why not become a zookeeper? Is another question I'm often asked. A zookeeper is a great job but it wasn't for me either. Many don't realize that a zookeeper must have a minimum of a Bachelors degree in biology in order to get an entry level position in any accredited zoo. As I have stated, science was never a strong subject of mine. Although zookeepers love their charges and spend lots of time with them, they do not own them and are not allowed to take them home. Due to the fact that I own my animals, I can bring them anywhere I like, whether it is a school, photo shoot, TV shoot, bar mitzvah or any of the other events I perform at each year.

Instead, I decided to take a different path: teaching. I graduated from a tiny little college on Long Island, called St. Joseph's College. It took me a little over four years to earn three degrees: one in general education, one in special education, and another in speech communications. All the while, I was applying for permit after permit to own everything from alligators to cobras to lions and tigers. I find it very impressive that I was able to start and operate a business, work two other jobs, complete my student teaching, write a thesis, and complete three separate bachelor degrees in only four and a half years; to this day I still marvel that I was able to do it all in that short time frame. For a long time I thought that my true calling in life was to be a teacher. After all, teaching was a normal, respectable, nine-to-five job. I figured I could always add the animals to my classroom as time went on. But just as I achieved my New York State teaching licenses, the market for teachers began to wane. I began Animal Adventures while in my freshman year of college as a hobby (because I never thought I could make a living doing it full time). However, upon my graduation from college I began to do extensive research on small business and absorbed four years of business school within several months of self instruction. With that research (and a leap of faith) I decided to give it a go. From that moment on I have completely enveloped myself in my passion, which is something very few people in this world can say they have done. I could never picture myself working with only twenty five students for ten months out of the year; through Animal Adventures I can reach over ten thousand children every year! My philosophy is that life is too short to be stuck doing something you don't like.

Chapter 1

Grandfathers and Grand Fish

I don't know what it is about grandfathers and fish but the two go together like peanut butter and jelly. Grandfathers either like to fish or they like to keep fish. Or in the case of my grandfather, Marco, they like both. I received my first fish tank when I was five years-old. I remember my grandfather coming over every week with shopping bags from the pet store containing bags of fish. Each week it would be a different species of freshwater fish, from danios to angelfish to discus to tetras to swordtails to mollies to snails. I feel so blessed to have been so young and to have someone so loving in my family who shared my passion with me. He taught me what fish liked to live at the top level of the tank and what fish preferred to live at the bottom. He taught me how to let new fish float in their bags at the top of the tank for several hours before being released into the tank.

My Grandfather is also an accomplished fisherman. He has always been the grandfather with the boat. It is only fifteen feet long but at five years-old it appeared to be as big as the Titanic. He would often pick me up in his Ford Explorer (boat in tow) in early spring and off we would go to spend the day fishing. A grandfather fishing with his grandson; cliché I know. I will never forget the first fish I ever caught in the Long Island sound: a sea robin. For those of you unfamiliar with this species, it is a very odd-looking fish that has wing-like appendages and a loud croaking call that it will emit when threatened. I remember looking at this amazing creature and thinking that I had just caught the most unusual animal in the world. I immediately summoned my grandfather who responded, "Agh, a sea robin- throw it back." I reeled in my line and unhooked my fish. I must have been the only child who indentified the beginning of spring when he saw a SEA robin.

Chapter 2

The Young Animal Lover

People often ask me how old I was when my love for animals began. That is a hard question to answer because I cannot remember a time in my life when I was not surrounded by animals. I grew up in Setauket New York, on the north shore of Long Island. The area is known for being densely wooded, so it will come as no surprise that there was always a plethora of small wild animals that I would be in contact with. I remember being four years-old and collecting worms and pill bugs under the loose bricks of the patio. I would then sneak them inside and draw pictures of them while I carefully studied them. There was another occasion where I was kindergarten-age and a local landscaper brought over an Eastern Box turtle that he had found during one of his calls. I placed the turtle in my backyard and watched him for hours until he finally made a slow retreat back into the woods that surrounded our house.

It wasn't until I was nine or ten years old that I truly remember keeping my first real exotic pet. This "exotic" pet was an Australian White's tree frog that my mother had purchased for me from a local pet store. I set up a five gallon terrarium on our kitchen counter for him. I named him "Herman" and pampered him with the best care possible. I wedged a piece of driftwood in the upper half of the terrarium for him to perch on and I would feed him a few crickets every week (which he would eat with gusto). An interesting thing that I learned while studying Herman was that frogs do not chew with teeth; instead they must blink after grabbing good. While blinking, a frog's eye balls will sink below their sockets and into the mouth cavity and induce somewhat of a chewing motion-how cool!

But it was the tree frog's other unique ability that caught my mother by surprise late one night. I distinctly remember being woken up one night by my mother who was shrieking in the kitchen. I raced down stairs and found her laughing. Confused, I asked what had happened and she pointed to Herman. She went on to explain that he had just croaked loudly and violently five minutes before. I looked at Herman, who sat looking like the cat who had swallowed the canary. It wasn't until a few nights later when I was raiding the kitchen pantry that I was assaulted by the cacophony of loud barking sounds. A few years later, I learned that most species of tree frogs are nocturnal and that the males often call out to females in the wild. Poor Herman lived his whole life as a bachelor which resulted in many endless nocturnal calls to girl frogs who didn't even exist! From Herman, my collection expanded and branched out to include larger reptiles, birds, guinea pigs, rabbits and eventually truly exotic wildlife.

Chapter 3:

"Uncle" Marc Morrone

Being an animal lover from such a young age, I would watch Discovery Channel and Animal Planet for hours on end as a child. I would watch anything I could find on TV that concerned animals. One day in elementary school I remember returning home and turning on the television. There, before my eyes, was this very intelligent man with thick glasses standing behind a table that was absolutely saturated with animals. I didn't know it at the time, but this man would soon become one of the most influential people in my life. His name was Marc Morrone, a long island pet store owner whose knowledge of animals had landed him on his own daily television program. Every day he would speak about pet care during the thirty minute show. I was immediately intrigued as the animals were often loose on a table in front of him, all happily interacting and playing with one another. I soon found myself racing to the television set everyday to watch Marc and his colorful menagerie. There were rabbits, ferrets, puppies, fish, and a gigantic Scarlet macaw parrot who would sit atop Marc's shoulders.

About a year later, my mother was speaking with a friend of hers who, through pure serendipity, mentioned one day that she grew up next door to a now-famous animal expert: Marc Morrone! This friend of my mother's promptly sent him an email telling him about me. Marc in turn went ahead and set up a meeting at his pet store with me. A few weeks later, I left with my mother and we drove for about an hour. We arrived in the town of Rockville Center. We walked to a store front with a green awning and I immediately realized where we were: *Parrots of the World*

(Marc's pet store). I have never again experienced the flurry of emotions that swept though my body at that moment. We walked through the store where I saw a large pen lined with shredded paper. Buried in all that paper was a huge Flemish Giant rabbit, made famous by Marc's show. We then walked into a glass-walled room that literally had hundreds of parrots in it (after all the name of the store was *Parrots of the World*). Against one corner was a very large wrought iron cage containing the beautiful Scarlet macaw parrot. If there is one thing that has earned Marc immortality it would have to be that large parrot on his shoulder, tugging at his glasses. Next to Harry, in a cage just as large, was Marc's ominous-looking African Raven who was well known on TV for grabbing fan mail and "filing" it by crumpling it up in his beak and discarding it on the floor. The only star missing was Marc

Morrone, but where was he? I soon spotted a very tall man with glasses cleaning out a fish tank: it was him! My star struck nature got the best of me and I froze. My mother walked up to him and introduced her and me. I shook his hand and he immediately asked me what types of animals I had. He went on to show me how each animal in the store was kept and cared for. Before leaving, I decided to grab a few animal supplies from various locations in the store and Marc was nice enough to throw in a pet care book, free of charge. Before we left he said, "Because we've finally met and you're my biggest fan, you can call me 'Uncle' Marc from now on." The meeting with him only took twenty minutes but it changed my life forever.

Chapter 4

On the Air with Marc Morrone

Several months after meeting Marc, a producer for Martha Stewart Living called my parents and informed them that they thought it would be cute to do a "Mini" Marc Morrone segment for the show. Apparently Marc was very impressed with my knowledge of the species held in his store and was the one responsible for pitching the idea to the producers over at Martha Stewart Living. As one could imagine, I was over the moon when my mother told me this.

The following week I loaded all of my animals up and off to Westport Connecticut my father and I went. Even at thirteen years-old, I had amassed quite the menagerie. Ferrets, guinea pigs, a chinchilla, turtles, small parrots, and a duck; all in pristine health due to care tips dispensed by Marc on his TV show.

Luckily I lived in near the maritime community of Port Jefferson at the time. This small town is on the north shore of Long Island and runs a ferry directly to Connecticut. We arrived at the studio (menagerie in tow) and were immediately surrounded by a very large estate. We made our way to a beautiful stone wall and wrought iron gates. After being buzzed in, my father parked his car and we began unloading my little zoo. Marc was immediately there in the parking lot, ready help grab cages and carry them into the studio. I have always been enamored with Marc for his ability and willingness to do the dirty work (which others in this industry often delegate to others). Once settled in, we were met by a producer, Jocelyn, who was clearly an animal lover and began asking me questions about my odd hobby. She handed me a script that highlighted the important points of the segment. She made a point of telling me that it was more of an outline than a true script as all they really wanted was to capture a fun conversation between Marc and myself. I read it over and changed into my wardrobe provided to me by the MSL stylists (by this point I was definitely feeling like a hot shot). The producers situated my animals adjacent to Marc's and on the cameras went! From the second the cameras began taping the script went out the window. Marc and I began to have a conversation about our love for the natural word and TV magic was formed. I must have done something right that day at thirteen years-old because that segment has gone viral and will pop up a thousand times over on any Google search under "Marc Morrone" or "Martha Stewart".

Chapter 5

Pedal to the Metal in New York City

Driving into New York City requires a certain skill set that few possess. You must be daring, creative, and have very good reflexes to do it right. I am proud to say that I have mastered the skill set. I credit my New York City driving abilities to my beloved animals. About a dozen or so times every year I am forced to drive into the city with them. Many of my animals are also shipped to me from zoos all over the world to airports located right in the city's center. Through no fault of my own, many of my adventures somehow always manage to position me in the city at the worst possible time.

I always wanted a raptor for my shows and decided on a beautiful Lanner falcon. These beautiful birds originate in Northern Africa and are a large bird at about two feet long. They have beautiful markings, enabling them to survive in an arid desert environment, right down to their football player-like eye black underneath each eye. I purchased my falcon from an accomplished falconer in upstate New York, who spent his free time raising and selling these beautiful birds to fellow falconers, zoos, and wildlife educators.

The day my falcon was ready to be picked up, I received a phone call from the breeder who informed me that he accidently delivered my bird to a nature center in the Bronx. This actually shortened the drive for me so I was happy to commute the fifty minutes to the Bronx as I would have otherwise had to drive all the way upstate. The only catch: it was my first time driving from Long Island to the Bronx and I was a little apprehensive. If that wasn't enough, on this particular day there was a fire on the Throgs Neck

Bridge (the bridge that connects Long Island to the Bronx) and traffic was then being diverted to the White Stone Bridge (the only other bridge that connects Long Island to the Bronx). This added five hours to the otherwise forty-five minute drive. I then found myself west-bound on the Long Island Expressway in a waltz-like motion where I would drive three feet, then stop for ten minutes, driving four feet, then stop for twenty minutes, driving for six feet, then stop for thirty minutes. This went on for about five hours.

I finally arrived in the parking garage of the nature center and pulled out my cell phone to tell my contact that I had arrived. That was until I heard quick siren and saw red lights in my rear-view mirror: a police officer was pulling me over! The officer came to my driver side, asked for my license and registration, and asked why I was on my cell phone. I explained the situation to him and told him that I was an animal handler picking up a new animal for my programs. I also told him that I had just been stuck in traffic for the past six hours. I also flashed one of my numerous PBA cards that had been given to me from law enforcement friends. Did I get the ticket? You bet! I then pulled out of that garage with a hefty ticket and a lower opinion of the NYPD.

Chapter 6

On the Air with College Humor

I am frequently asked to appear on TV and other venues to speak as a wildlife consultant. One of the earliest experiences I had with this was when I received a call from a company called Collegehumor.com. I was in my office one day, doing paper work for my permits, when my phone rang.

"Animal shows, this is Nick," I answered in my scripted telephone greeting.

"Hi I work for College Humor and was on your website and would like to have you on a segment we're filming tonight at one o'clock in the morning."

Half thinking that this was a prank call I immediately responded, "Sure I can do that, what animals would you like to use?" This person went on to explain that he they were making a late night talk show parody and would be streaming it live from a residential apartment. I agreed and was off to Brooklyn. I met the producer that had hired me outside of an apartment along with other "cast members" that they had hired for this particular segment. They consisted of a six member band, a Broadway actor who would be playing the host, as well as a cast member from *30 Rock*. Here we all stood, a dozen or so misfits from all walks of entertainment, waiting to barge into an apartment in the middle of the night. I was then quietly guided into the building carrying four crates filled with animals. I was told to wait in the hall until one of the producers ushered me in. My cue was when the announcer said my name. I immediately came into the room carrying a kangaroo, monkey, and parrot. I was instructed to act as a Jim Fowler-type of animal expert (think back to the Seinfeld episode where Kraemer thinks he's Merv Griffin). The segment went very well and the producers were so cordial and said they were so happy to have me on with them.

A few weeks later I received a call from my struggling actor and screenwriter of a brother, Jordan who resides in Los Angeles.

"Did you know you're on IMDB?"

"What's IMDB?" I immediately asked.

Apparently IMDB (the "Internet Movie Data Base") is a very well known data base for actors, screen writers, directors and anyone else related to entertainment. Jordan informed me that it is very hard to be listed on this particular website, as professional actors must perform in several credible shows or movies before you placed on it. So there I was: the crazy animal guy from New York who made it to IMDB in one night.

Chapter 7

The Cat and Matt (Lauer)

Many throughout the world have heard of a group of towns located on Long Island's south fork: The Hamptons. The same Hamptons that is known as a playground for the rich and famous. I happen to live about forty minutes away from these towns and have been hired by a prestigious summer camp located in the heart of it all for the past several years. I knew it would only be a matter of time before one of the children went home talking about me to their famous parents who would then in turn hire me for their swanky events and their children's birthday parties.

This worked ten-fold when I picked up my phone one day in November.

"Hi Nick? This is Matt Lauer, I heard you do a great animal show."

I nearly fell off my desk chair when I heard this. Matt then informed me that he would love to have me perform at his son's sixth birthday party.

The morning of the event I was a mess. I gave all of the animals a pep talk about how important it was to make a good impression (I'm sure that was very productive). I had all hands on deck to pack the van. From kangaroos and monkeys to alligators and pythons to foxes and parrots and toucans, they were all ready to go with me to the Lauer home. Upon arrival, I was met by a large wrought iron gate and was beeped in (I began to have flash backs of Martha Stewart's Estate). I then drove down a very long, winding path until finally arriving at the facade of a gorgeous Victorian home. There at the front door was he himself: Matt Lauer: looking just as polished and poised as he does on *The Today Show* He then shook my hand and introduced himself. He then showed me the space in the back of the house that he was planning on using for my little performance. I informed him it would be about ten minutes for me to set up and at that point he could "sic" the children on me. As I was setting up my tables and equipment I began to feel as if I was being watched. I then slowly pivoted to a small bush I saw in the corner of my eye. Sure enough, I could see orange glowing eyes glaring back at me and me out pops a beautiful Abyssinian cat (a rare breed, once prized by the Ancient Egyptians). This cat studied me and went on with his business as he leapt in and out of his bush as I continued to set up my equipment. Five minutes before the children were ready to descend, Matt again came out and to check on me and immediately spotted his cat and tried to retrieve it. At this point I assumed he would summon a nanny or grounds keeper to get the cat but, to my surprise, he climbed into the bush and began reaching in. All the while he was wearing, what I assume, were custom tailored pants and cashmere pull-over. After another five minutes of branch rustling he emerged scruffing the cat by the neck which he immediately tossed back into the house. Without a minute to spare, the fifteen children flooded outside and surrounded my table where I put on one of the best shows I can remember. Upon completion of his son's show, Matt met me in the front of his home and emphatically thanked me for coming out to do this for him. As I drove away, I was flabbergasted by how normal this man truly was. Fame and fortune had clearly never jaded him. I can honestly say that the Matt Lauer that appears on *The Today Show* every morning in millions of households throughout the country is the real deal.

Chapter 8

FURgetaboutit

I was always a huge fan of HBO's *The Sopranos*. I would rush home on Sunday nights during the years it ran. I am a huge fan of anything "Mafia" and loved the colorful characters that were depicted on the show every week. So when I was asked to appear with Joseph R. Gannascoli (who played "Vito" on the series) on a new reality TV show I didn't hesitate. Apparently he lived very close to me, right on Long Island and I was asked to provide a few exotic animals that would be featured on the show.

The day of the taping, I brought two wallabies, an alligator, a few birds, and a monkey. I was star struck when Joseph walked on the set. I immediately felt as if I was in the presence of a modern-day *Mafioso*. As he opened his mouth and began to speak with everyone else on the set, I realized he was just a typical New York guy who apt to make wisecracks. He walked over to a crew member who was mounting a teleprompting screen under his camera. The screen measured about three feet wide by two feet high. Joseph immediately remarked, "Hey that's too small, how am I supposed to read that?" He then looked at my transport crates and I braced myself for, what I thought, would be a flurry of animal-related jokes (something I'm all too familiar with). Instead, he asked what types of animals I brought and what I do for a living. He seemed very sincere and intrigued. I showed him the animals and took out one of my favorites, Russell, the wallaby, and showed him to Joseph, who then started gently stroking his head. Once I saw that he was nothing like his blood-thirsty character, Vito, I decided to ask if he would be willing to take a picture with me. He obliged and patiently waited while I handed the camera to my assistant and propped up the little wallaby in my arms. I was very pleased with how it came out and thanked him profusely. It is now one of the first images prospective clients see when they log onto my website. The rest of the filming went great and I was soon dismissed. However, upon returning to my van, I began trembling as I started the ignition; nerves I was sure, but why? Possibly the exhilaration at meeting a prominent celebrity, or possibly I was grateful not to have been "whacked"!

Chapter 9

Lions, Tigers, and Bears, Oh My!

Every animal trainer, if they are honest, will tell you that the main reason they went into such a field was to look impressive handling a large predator like a lion or tiger. We have all grown up watching cartoon caricatures of lion tamers or safari guides on TV and I was no different. I dreamed of one day working with these large and amazing animals.

When I was twenty years-old I was introduced to a local animal trainer who routinely used lion and tigers for print ads in New York City. Before I knew it, he was allowing me to rent his animals for my shows. I would bring home eight week-old tiger and lion cubs and play mom (father lions and tigers don't play much of a role in the direct care of their young). I learned that tigers will immediately "chuff" back to mom and to their favorite human handlers. Chuffing if a sound that is a combination of a purr and a trilled Spanish "R". I learned that both lions and tigers have a predatory drive from the moment they are born. When you see baby lions and tigers jumping on each other in a zoo it may look cute, but they are actually doing this to practice taking down prey as adults. These little animals would stalk me as I moved around the kitchen preparing formula for them. It was amazing to see them think and problem solve. I could see the wheels turning in their mind as they figured out the distance between me and them and deciphered if I was small enough for them to jump on and overtake. Pound for pound, big cats are very strong; much stronger than a similarly sized dog. The female Bengal tiger I worked with during those months was only eighteen pounds and could easily bring me to my knees when she jumped and bit my legs. I also learned that lions and tigers require special supplementation in their diets. Like our household cats, they require various vitamins and minerals in their diet, such as Taurine and Calcium. Deficiencies of such vitamins could result in poor eyesight and stunted bones. I loved those lions and tigers but the day finally came at the end of that summer when I had to say good bye.

I knew I couldn't keep them long-term as such animals require expansive habitats which I knew I could never provide in my small facility. I still remember saying goodbye to them as they were loaded into large metal crates and placed in the back of a specialized trailer. Both are now full grown and live in a beautiful zoo in North Carolina. They live in a fenced acre complete with palm trees and a water fall. Every once in a while I will drive down to visit with them and am in awe every time I do. They are now so large that I can only visit with them behind a chain link fence. On my last visit the Asiatic Lion, Aslan, placed his paw against the fence. His pad alone was three times the size of his entire body when he was an eight week-old cub. The zoo hopes the lion and tiger will soon breed to create a rare and equally beautiful species, known as a Liger.

Chapter 10

The King of Queens

It was February of 2010 when I received a call from a frantic pet store owner in Queens looking to re-home a Patagonian Cavy. Before I continue, I'm assuming many of you reading have no idea what that is. The Patagonian Cavy is a large rodent from South America that can weigh up to thirty pounds and looks like a guinea pig on stilts. Back to my story, this pet store owner explained to me that he was in violation of the animal welfare act as he did not have a valid license to display this animal in his store. This man then asked if I would be willing to take this animal "off his hands." I agreed, and was soon on my way to Queens.

I arrived in the New York City borough an hour later and walked into the pet store. What I did not expect was the greeting I got! The staff immediately surrounded me and emphatically started thanking me for helping them. I then asked the store owner to bring me to the enclosure. He led me down a hallway which opened up into a larger section of the store. He had four, what appeared to be, Plexiglas shower stall-like animal enclosures all lined up and each containing different animals. One contained a toucan, another contained a pair of African ravens, another South American Porcupines, and the last contained the Patagonian Cavy I was there for. The store owner had found placements for the other animals in licensed zoos within the state. I then asked the employees who would be going into the enclosure to get the animal. They looked at me odd until one of the said, "You are." When you're an animal handler this type of thing is common, so I opened the door to the "shower stall" enclosure and brought the transport crate in with me. I was told that she had not been handled in four years and was not used to people. I opened the door to the crate and placed it at the wall of the enclosure. I then proceeded to "herd" her into the crate. I would do this by getting her to the side of the enclosure and spooking her to run into the crate. The reason I knew this would work is because the enclosure was circle shaped (not square shaped like many animal enclosures). This would allow her to run unencumbered without hitting corners. The plan went as expected and I was able to "herd" her into the crate and lock the door to it. The employees looked at me as if I had just slain a dragon. As I carried to now twenty pound crate to my van one of the employees exclaimed, "You brother, are the real King of Queens."

Chapter 11

The Almighty Alligator

The first permit that I received to possess a wild animal was an endangered species permit for an American Alligator. Alligators are illegal to own in the state of New York unless one has this particular permit. The permit allowed me to obtain one American Alligator for educational use. The permit dictated how the animal was to be housed and how the animal was to be obtained: out of state from a licensed dealer.

I followed every rule on the permit and received my first Alligator hatchling a few months later. "Gatorade" as I came to call him was truly an amazing animal. I used a large aquarium to house him in. One of the first things I learned about alligators is the fact that they have some of the toughest, most leathery skin of any reptile.

Gatorade helped me educate thousands of people during my shows.

In the summer time I housed Gatorade in a custom three hundred gallon pond in my backyard that I built myself. It had a small fence and cover to keep Gatorade from wandering out. One of the truly interesting things I found with Gatorade was that he literally became "wild" when he was housed in that pond. When inside his aquarium, he would let me do anything to him, but outside was a different story. When I needed to retrieve him from his pond for a show in the summer I would have to reach into the murky water until I felt a nip on my hand. Once he was clamped down, I would figure out where his tail was and hoist him from the pond. To get him to release my hand I would push in (this will cause any animal to reflexively let go of you if you're being bitten). I would then load him into his transport box and off we would go!

I had Gatorade for a little over two years before he grew too large to use in my shows (a little over four feet long). I knew the day would finally come when I would have to part with him and I found a nice home for him in a zoo in North Carolina that was seeking a male alligator for their two juvenile females. At around four feet long, I was glad that I didn't wait any later to place *that* alligator.

Chapter 12

Batty for Bats

An animal that had always escaped my grasp was a bat (and not for the reasons you may think!) These unique animals are extremely hard to find unless you are an accredited. I was always amazed that they are this planet's only flying mammals. I had read *Stellaluna* while in elementary school and had taught many lesson plans involving the story during my student teaching years. I knew I had to have one of my very own.

I received a call from another one of my many animal friends who operates an animal importation company out of a Long Island City warehouse. He had just received a shipment of one hundred Egyptian Fruit Bats that were going to be sent to zoos throughout the country. He was willing to give me a baby if I was willing to drive to the warehouse and pick one out. I jumped into my van and was off to Long Island City. First, I have to describe the warehouse. Picture a self storage warehouse, where there are separate garage-like cubicles. His animal warehouse looked very much like this. However, each of his "cubicles" housed a different species. In one cubicle that measured ten feet by twenty feet he had about eighty fruit bats ranging in sizes from four to eight inches in length. I was then instructed to walk into this cubicle that had all of these bats lazily fluttering around like butterflies. For most people this would have been a horrific request, but I knew that I was perfectly safe. This group was part of a long-term captive colony and they were used to people. Furthermore, bats never attack people; those old wives tales that say they get tangled in the hair of pretty girls are simply not true. I walked in to this cubicle and the bats immediately scattered. I then began the painstaking task of locating a baby that was only three to four months-old (one that I could train and get used to handling). I immediately turned and saw little "Igor" gripping to my sleeve. He was healthy, young, and already seemed very friendly toward people. I then gently scooped him up and placed him carefully into a plastic shoe box that was fitted with ventilation holes. Little Igor soon settled into his enclosure back at my facility and is now pivotal animal for my "Creatures of the Night" program that is available for schools and libraries during Halloween. Egyptian Fruit bats have a live span of over thirty years in captivity so I am sure that Igor will continue to be a vital part of Animal Adventures for many years to come.

Chapter 13

A Kinship with Kangaroos

We have all grown up reading *Winnie the Pooh* and wishing we could have our own "Kanga" or "Roo". This fantasy followed me into adulthood when I finally decided that my animal show would not be complete without a little "Roo" of my own. I soon found a zoo in Texas that had a surplus six month-old male Red kangaroo that they agreed to sell to me. My little kangaroo was then shipped to LaGuardia airport in a large dog crate; you wouldn't believe the looks I got in the cargo terminal when I went to pick him up!

I had "Lou" the kangaroo for a little over a month and he soon became one of my favorite animals. He would ride around in special made backpack and would always impress the children at the shows. Lou was still being bottle fed and three to four times a day I would have to prepare "kangaroo formula" that I had obtained from a zoo supply catalogue. Kangaroo formula was unlike any other type of animal formula I had ever used. It had the consistency of cake batter rather than milk and smelled very sweet. Lou was very unusual looking for a Red Kangaroo. Instead of the typical red coloring that is commonly associated with the species, he instead sported a gorgeous bluish gray color. This was because the zoo that had him before me had him neutered at a very young age to keep him from fighting with other male kangaroos as he got older. Not only did this procedure give him a beautiful coat but it also made him extremely gentle. I housed Lou in an outdoor chain link enclosure that measured ten feet square. He had lots of room to hop around and do other kangaroo things. He was growing very well and getting bigger within the month I had him...until one fateful day.

At the time, I was a junior in college and was still living at home with my parents where the animals outdoors. Back in those days, I would run home in between classes to check on the animals before having to rush back out to my college where I would have class well into the night. On this particular day it was a quick visual inspection of all the animals. I checked everyone inside the main barn, no problems there. I then checked the adjacent chain link enclosure that housed Lou and I noticed he was laying on his side. This was nothing out of the ordinary as it is a common posture for both kangaroos in the wild and in captivity. Kangaroos are desert animals and have evolved to conserve energy and keep cool by lying on their sides when not hopping around. I then called him expecting him to hop over to the fence and give me a kiss. "Here Lou, I have your bottle," I called. Lou raised his head up at me but didn't hop over and I immediately knew something was wrong. I rushed into the enclosure to get a closer to look. To my horror, his hind leg was tangled in the chain link of his enclosure. I immediately untangled his leg, hoping he would go back to jumping around. He didn't move at all. I then rushed to the main barn and grabbed his backpack. I then carefully put him into his pouch and made my way to my car as I dialed a local veterinarian on my cell phone. Adrenaline must have kicked in because I distinctly remember trying to walk over to my car do and not being able to do so. I felt like I was in a nightmare running towards something I needed and my legs were turning to *jell-o*. Luckily my brother, Jordan, had just arrived home and I was able to tell him what had happened. He immediately made room for me and Lou in his car and off we went. I remember feeling very relieved that Jordan drove a Japanese sports car as we were able to make it to the local veterinary clinic within twenty minutes (normally a forty minute drive in my van). I immediately rushed Lou inside where a technician was waiting to take him in. About ten minutes later she came out and ushered us into the x-ray room. The veterinarian entered and explained to me that one of Lou's back bones was completely crushed; euthanasia was the only option. Tears began to stream down my face and I remember looking over and seeing Jordan crying also. Lou was still under sedation from the x-ray when I went into the room. I picked up his head and was flooded with different emotions. First sadness, then anger at myself for housing him in such a dangerous enclosure, then despair for having to euthanize such a beautiful, young animal. On the ride home I cursed myself for bringing these animals into this world and I seriously contemplated giving up Animal Adventures. I'll never forget what Jordan said, "Nick, accidents like these are bound to happen. I'm sorry you lost Lou today, but it helps you learn and become a better animal keeper. You cannot deprive the kids your special show. No one in the world can do it like my big brother." Jordan had never said anything so prophetic before and I immediately realized how much he admired me for what I do. Working with animals isn't always easy. It requires compassion, dedication, love, and a heart that is bound to be broken every now and then.

Chapter 14

Jack Frost Nipping at Your Nose

Another story involving a kangaroo was when a zoo in Rome, New York called me begging me to take their three year-old albino kangaroo. I jumped at the opportunity as albino animals are typically very rare and highly sought after. They even offered to deliver him to Long Island (a six hour trip each way for them). It never occurred to me that there might be a reason why they wanted to be rid of him so badly.

Within two days of him being at my facility I realized what the reason was: he was extremely aggressive. As soon as I would open the door to his enclosure he would grab my arm and start the stereotypical "boxing" behavior typical of the species. He would grab my arm, balance on his thick tail, and drop kick me with his massive feet. Many times he succeeded in kicking me completely onto the ground and knocking the wind out of me. He would also bite me very hard from time to time (this is very unusual for kangaroos). I named my newest acquisition "Jack Frost" for his coloring and icy demeanor. In truth, he was actually a wallaby. Wallabies are the smaller cousins of kangaroos and are typically full grown at around three feet tall and about forty-five pounds. But Jack Frost was a true freak of nature. He stood almost five feet-tall and weighed in at around seventy-five pounds. Interestingly enough, he quickly became a very popular animal during my shows.

I worked around Jack's ornery personality by training him to wear a harness attached a leash. When I say train, I really mean that I got him to tolerate it. The trick was getting it on him. I would slowly sneak up to his cage with the harness tucked behind me and out of sight. I would then call him over and offer him his favorite treat: an apple wedge with a little bit of peanut butter. He would immediately snatch the apple with his hand-like paws and drool all over it. While he was engrossed with his snack, I would take a deep breath and leap on his back. During the rodeo that would inevitably ensue, I would somehow work his torso into the harness and strap him in.

After six months, I decided to part ways with Jack. I felt he would be happier in larger quarters so I decided to put a call into a friend of mine who runs a zoo in Oklahoma. He was very receptive and agreed to take Jack because he had a lone female wallaby that needed a mate. Jack has been there for many years now and has since fathered several baby wallabies. Just like dad, one was even born pure white!

Chapter 15

My House, My Habitat

One of the great challenges that faced me when I graduated college was where I would live. Although I loved my parents, I didn't want to live with them anymore. Most people my age would have opted to rent an apartment until they could afford a house. However, my animals prevented this from being a viable option. Even though I had money saved and had a lucrative business to support me, this still was not enough to place a down payment for a home on Long Island (which can be very expensive).

My family decided to dispatch my grandmother who was a very successful realtor and asked her what she thought. She immediately recalled seeing a small beautiful home for sale that was located on the north shore of Long Island. It was being offered for sale by a local bank that had foreclosed on its previous owners. When she brought me over to see the house I was astonished. It had brand new appliances, brand new carpeting, and a separate apartment in the basement. It was also walking distance to the beach! If that wasn't enough, the backyard contained a twenty by twenty foot barn that looked as if it was a guest home once upon a time. I knew this would be the animal new barn. The price for such a great home was less than half of what homes in the area usually went for. It seemed that the bank wanted to get rid of the house as soon as possible. I moved in within the next few months and slowly converted the guest house into a state-of-the-art animal housing facility complete with full spectrum lighting, built-in enclosures, heating, air conditioning, running water, and a refrigerator. I can truly say that I love my home. If I won the lottery tomorrow, I wouldn't leave. The house itself is small, as it was originally designed to be a beach bungalow in the 1950's. Its main purpose was to serve as a weekend or summer retreat for New York City residents who could not afford the ritzier areas on the Gold Coast of Long Island which, in my opinion, adds to its charm.

Chapter 16

Killer Kinkajous

There is a small raccoon-like animal that inhabits the jungles of South America that awakes at night: the kinkajou. They are small animals with a light brown coat and an insatiable craving for fruit. Their appearance is misleading as they look very much like monkeys. In South America they are called "honey bears" for their love of honey and their striking resemblance to a streamlined teddy bear. Paris Hilton made them very famous when she purchased one as a personal pet and named it "Baby Love".

I obtained my first pair of kinkajous from a breeder in Oregon. I used them for several months as they were incredibly tame. I named the male "Fondue" and the little female "Honey". One day I received a call from one of my employees when I was out doing a program. She said that the female had severely bitten her. When I got home, her hand was extremely swollen and bore four puncture marks from Honey's sharp teeth. Thankfully, she made a full recovery.

I shrugged off the entire incident until a few weeks later when I found myself in the animal barn to feed everyone. Keep in mind, this was in the middle of winter and I was wearing a very thick leather jacket. I opened the door to the kinkajou cage (which was over ten feet tall) to drop a few pieces of fruit and marshmallows into the cage. Usually they would wait until after I was done before descending to the bottom of the cage to enjoy their dinner. On this particular day I opened the cage door and saw a blur of brown fur zip past my face and I immediately felt a pinching pain on my under arm. It felt like my arm had just been hit with thirty needles and then clamped in a vice. I had to pry Honey off of my arm until she decided a banana would taste better. Later that night I took a look at my arm and to my surprise there were several inch-long gashes that were still bleeding! Bear in mind, I was wearing a thick leather jacket when this happened.

I would later find out from other animal trainers that kinkajous are extremely difficult to work with once they reach adulthood and must be neutered or spayed to prevent aggression. Anyone who works with me on a professional level knows that I take public safety very seriously. Part of my responsibility as an exotic animal handler is to keep those attending my shows safe at all times.

I soon decided that both kinkajous would be better situated in a more natural setting. Once spring came that year, I relocated both kinkajous to a fantastic animal sanctuary in Florida. I still get updates from the sanctuary director (a close friend of mine) who states they are a visitor favorite. The two of them have a much larger outdoor enclosure that is set in the woods of central Florida. Who else can say they received a Florida retirement when they were fired?

Pinocchio the Coatimundi

Leona the lemur

My resident monkeys, Abu and Tarzan

Training a seven month-old Bengal Tiger Cub

Posing with Matt Lauer

Agatha, a South American Agouti

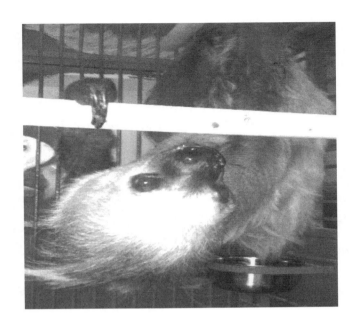

"Clawdia" the toe toed sloth

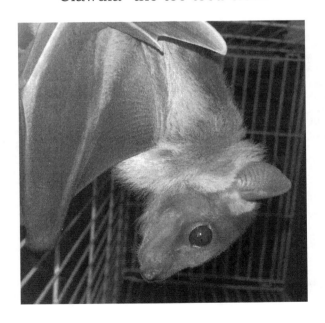

Igor the Fruit Bat

Gatorade the Alligator

Cheesecake the Burmese Python

Chapter 17

Agatha the Agouti

I am constantly asked what the worst injury was that I have ever sustained while caring for my animals. Part of the reason that I am able to prevent serious injury is that I do not own any animals that are over fifty pounds. Nor do I possess any venomous animals. Even though I am constantly being kicked, scratched, and bitten (I usually have several fresh scratches on my arms or hands at any one time) I rarely scar. For some reason, my body has a remarkable ability to heal deep punctures in a matter of days. That being said, there was one time when I did scar and it came from a nasty bite.

I was cleaning the cage of my newly imported agouti (a South American rodent that weighs about twenty-five pounds and is closely related to the guinea pig). She was extremely skittish and detested being handled. I later found out that she was wild caught in Brazil at six months-old and shipped to a zoo in Texas that couldn't use her. I named her "Agatha" after one of my favorite writers: Agatha Christie (I assure you the alliteration was pure coincidence!).

Training her to accept handling was a nightmare. I would have to grab her and place her in an open basket that was lined with hay. I would then throw in banana slices and raisins in it (her favorite treats). I would then go about my cleaning duties for the other animals. On one particular day I grabbed Agatha and she decided to sink her three inch-long teeth into my thumb. It is probably worth noting that the only other animal that has the jaw strength of an agouti is the Hyacinth Macaw (the largest parrot on Earth). I distinctly remember her top teeth being sunk in about a centimeter below my thumb nail and her bottom teeth sunk cleanly on the other side of my thumb. When she finally let go my entire thumb was completely sliced open. With me being the tough guy that I am, I didn't tell anyone. I simply rinsed it with peroxide. The wound healed completely within two weeks. It is the only bite that ever scarred and I still have a mark on my left thumb. The worst animal injury I ever had: a bite from a twenty-five pound rat!

Chapter 18

Adios Amigo

A few years ago I had a nine-banded armadillo that I had acquired from a zoo dealer in Florida. I promptly named him "Amigo" as the word "Armadillo" is also Spanish (meaning "little armored one"). The alliteration was just icing on the cake! I marveled at how heavy and robust my new acquisition was. He had thick reptile-like skin complete with the indicative armored plating on the back (many scientists even believe that armadillos are the missing link between mammals and reptiles).

I decided that he would be right at home in a large terrarium that had a screen lid. Upon arrival in his new habitat, he seemed content and immediately went to sleep under a pile of pine wood shavings that had been placed in there for him. The next morning I went into the animal building to find the armadillo missing from his terrarium. Not only that, but the entire terrarium was knocked over and the entire area was in complete disarray. At that moment I remembered that armadillos are nocturnal and are most active at night. He must have gotten bored once night fell and pushed his way out to explore his new surroundings. I eventually found him sleeping in a bag of shredded paper that was used as bedding for the other animals.

I then decided to move onto plan B. I found a large wire rabbit cage that was about six feet long. It had horizontal wires that made up its frame. I placed Amigo in it and within seconds he used his armadillo strength and tiny mouth to bend the wire just enough to push his whole body through. I felt like I was watching *King Kong.*

OK, on to plan C I thought. Instead of housing him in a glass terrarium or wire cage I assumed he would be more comfortable in a more spacious pen. The pen that I had in mind measured eight feet long and five feet deep. It was an open-top design and had three foot tall walls that were lined with wire mesh. Even though it was an open top, I knew that armadillos are terrestrial animals that could not climb. The next morning I went into the animal building to see everything as it should be. That is for one small detail: Amigo was missing yet again! I immediately thought he had vanished. But sure enough, I walked over to the bag of shredded paper and there he was, sleeping. But how? Did he leap out of the pen the previous night? I immediately grabbed him and tossed him back into the pen. A few seconds later he did an about face and walked right up to the pen wall. What he did next left me in awe. Had I not seen it with my own eyes I never would have believed it. He rested his front legs on the wire mesh and began to climb up the wall like a mountain climber ascending Mt. Everest. The little armadillo was pushing his nails deep into a section of mesh as a foot hold and would then push to reach a higher section, eventually repeating the whole process until he scaled the wall. Similar to the stabbing motion a mountain climber will make with his set of picks which carry him up as he pulls. I had never read that armadillos were capable of such behavior. This was a great example of how first-hand experience is life's greatest teacher. There are some things you simply can't learn in books. I finally found a large stock tank that was originally designed as a water dish for horses and cows to drink from. It measured eight feet long and had three foot high solid sides (with no wire mesh foot holds). That was when I was finally able to solve the problem of *Adios* Amigo!

Chapter 19

The Snake Escape

Anyone who has seen my shows will most likely see my impressive Burmese Python (known by his fans as "Cheesecake the snake"). He was donated to me by New York City animal control when they found him in a small, cold tank in an abandoned apartment in the Bronx. When he first came to live with me he was very thin and was about six feet long. Through the years he has put on weight and is now a beautiful eleven foot long specimen. He has a wonderful personality and is truly one of my favorite animals. That being said, he has one foible: he loves to escape!

His first escape occurred a few months after he came to live with me. At the time, he was housed in a large aquarium that had a locking screen lid. This "lock" was actually just a pair of clips that secured the screen to the rim of the aquarium. These clips are typically sold in pet stores and manufactured for containing small reptiles and other small animals inside glass aquariums. However, they were no match for the pure muscle and brawn of a determined Burmese Python. For several days in a row I would enter my reptile building to find Cheesecake's aquarium lid ajar and Cheesecake nowhere in sight. I would always find him a few feet away, either sunning himself in the windowsill or coiled up in front of the building's heater.

The second time he escaped he caught me completely off guard. It was several years ago and I was scheduled for four consecutive shows, all at different corners of Long Island. The hectic schedule had me driving back and forth on the Long Island Expressway throughout the day. I had just packed up after my second show of the day and was headed back out to do the third. As I made my way east, I checked my speed and decided to reduce it. As I eased my foot onto the brake pedal I noticed that it wouldn't go all the way down. Being in the frantic mindset that I was in, I kept my eyes on the road and assumed it was just another minor repair that would have to be tended to the following day. Forty minutes later I began to feel my gas pedal rising and it eventually raised my foot off of it (and of course causing my van to slow down on the congested roadway). This time the issue got my attention and I immediately looked down to see what was going on: there was Cheesecake weaving in between the gas and brake pedals! Well in fact, it was the first third of his body, the rest of his body was stretched out underneath my seat, with his tail sticking out in the rear of the van. I am sure that if I had been anyone else in that situation that I would have caused a major car accident that day. But knowing what I did about snakes and about Cheesecake, I assumed he was merely trying to get warm. I slowly pulled into the nearest park and ride, uncoiled my serpentine passenger from under the seat and placed him back in to his travel box. As I did so, I received many honks and odd looks from Long Island commuters who were making their way back from work that day. I'm sure they were trying to figure out what in the world I was doing; I must have looked like someone losing a game of tug-o-war as I yanked the yellow "rope" from the driver side of my van.

I have been able to curtail Cheesecake's Houdini-like antics in recent times by providing him with a *locking* travel box (complete with a heat pad) and by housing him in a large, *padlocked* zoo-grade snake cage (complete with large heating elements). But you never know, he may decide to back "slide" into his old ways and make a surprise appearance at the wrong part of my show. So if you plan on seeing one of my shows in the future, you have been forewarned!

Chapter 20

The Ring-tailed Escape Artist

An uncommon animal that is commonly kept by many animal trainers is another relative of the raccoon called the "coatimundi" or simply "coati." It is about the same size as a raccoon but has a longer nose. He still sports the ringtail associated with his North American cousin. Unlike a true raccoon, coatimundis have a nice temperament which makes them a great show animal; I knew I had to have one.

Soon after deciding on such an interesting species, I decided to stop in to Uncle Marc's to pick up some animal supplies. Over the years Marc and I have developed a special type of friendship, one where you can read a person's energy and know exactly what they're thinking. This being said, I walked into Marc's store one day and spotted him in between phone calls and hand-feeding baby parrots.

"Nick, do you want a coatimundi? I'm importing group from Texas next week"

"Yes, as a matter of fact, I do!"

Sure enough, one week later he had my eight week-old coatimundi waiting for me. This little animal was only about the size of a guinea pig and squeaking away when Marc placed him into my transport box. "Pinocchio" as I named him has gone on to become a very popular show animal.

He is one of the smartest animals I have ever had and can learn a trick in less than five minutes. This keen intelligence may have saved his life two years after I bought him. In the summer time I like to allow my animals to live outside to enjoy fresh air and sunshine. Pinocchio was no exception. I constructed a beautiful chain link enclosure for him that measured six feet square. He enjoyed his enclosure and played in it daily until one fateful day. The enclosure was adjacent to my home office and I would routinely look out the window to check on Pinocchio as I would check emails and answer phone calls. If he was out of sight all that I needed to do was tap on my window and he would pop out and look at me. On this particular day I looked outside and didn't see him in his enclosure. I tapped on the glass: nothing. Another tap: nothing. I then ran outside and my heart sank when I realized Pinocchio was not in the enclosure, but how? When I examined the enclosure I realized that there was a ten inch opening on the top; more than enough for a determined coatimundi to fit through. But it didn't matter how he had gotten out, he was gone and wouldn't be coming back any time soon.

Complicating the situation is that fact that I live in the middle of the woods in Eastern Long Island. Even if I wanted to search for him, I wouldn't even know where to begin. I ran back to my office and printed out one hundred flyers with Pinocchio's picture on it and a brief description of what he is and why I have him. I also included a disclaimer that he wasn't dangerous in any way shape or form (the last thing I needed was the alarm my neighbors). Several hours past and night began to fall. Right when I had given up hope my cell phone rang and, sure enough, it was the call I was hoping for. Apparently Pinocchio was only one block east sitting high up in a neighbor's tree. My neighbor told me he seen my flyer and told his two young daughters to be on the look-out. Sure enough Pinocchio chose their yard to play in when he decided to crash the tea party that his daughters were having. I arrived at his house within two minutes, armed with a net, a trap, and the most effective weapon: smooth peanut butter (Pinocchio's favorite treat). My relief again turned to despair after I had arrived at the neighbor's house and realized just how high up he really was. My little friend was frantically waving his ring-tail back and forth like a castaway's S.O.S. signal. I then looked at my watch and realized the sun would completely set in another ten minutes. With a leap of faith, I looked down and opened the jar, hoping the smell of the peanut butter would emanate to where my little friend was. Coatimundis have one of the best noses in the animal world and have been known to smell out food up to two miles away in their natural ranges of Central and South America. I looked up again and there was Pinocchio, up-side-down making his way down the tree. He eventually made his way down to my shoulders and gave me his typical coatimundi hug. Every once in a while I'll get a call from that neighbor exclaiming that there was a sale on peanut butter. I always respond, "Come on over, Pinocchio would love some."

Chapter 21

Slowly, Slowly, Goes the Sloth

One of the oddest animals that I have ever had the pleasure of working with was a two toed sloth. These unique animals are found high in the canopy of the rainforest of South America. They move so slow that a unique species of moss grows only on their fur. Very few sloths are ever seen in zoos and fewer yet are seen in educational programs. This put the sloth high on my wish list.

I eventually located a female in a breeding facility in Oregon and made plans to have her shipped to New York. I was immediately enraptured by her uniqueness. I learned so many things in the short time that I had "Clawdia". I learned that when sloths sleep they curl their body into a tight circle the size of a beach ball. However, when climbing or reaching for something, they can easily stretch to over six feet from front claw to back claw. Feeding Clawdia was like being in the presence of an alien. Her favorite treat was a banana and she would climb right over to me as soon as she saw me with one. I would outstretch my arm with a banana and she would extend her right claw to then slowly snatch it. She would then "reel" the banana into her mouth and she would very slowly masticate it with her triangular fangs. Her eyes were small amber-colored buttons with small dark pupils. Even though they were small, they were incredibly expressive. After eating her banana she would get a sparkle in her eye and usually retreat to the top of her cage for a nap.

The most important lesson that the sloth taught me is to move slowly and to appreciate and life. When life if moving at a New York minute, all I have to do is close my eyes and think of Clawdia slowly gnawing on her banana, without a care in the world.

Chapter 22

Leona the Lemur

Many come in from zoos, either as babies or as retired exhibit animals. However, several years ago I received one animal in bit of a different way. I remember being on the phone with a friend of mine who operates a small zoo in the Catskill region of New York. He explained to me that he had an extra female lemur and that he would be more than happy to give her to me, the only catch: she was completely blind. I had an opening on my endangered species permit and had always wanted a lemur for my shows so I jumped at the chance.

One week later, I found myself driving to upstate New York from Long Island. Upon arrival I was met by a large winding dirt road in the woods that led to an expansive property with horses and other farm animals who studied my van intently as I pulled into the parking lot. My friend, John, who owned the zoo, waved me into the entrance. Although I had been in contact with him for many years this was the first that time I had actually been to the zoo. He explained that the lemur was in his office and that we would have to meander through the front of the zoo to get to it. As we walked, I passed many large pens, each containing a species more exotic than the last; from llamas to pigs to porcupines to owls to large carnivores. As I made my way past each animal I noticed something very peculiar: each animal had several tan noodles strewn about their habitats. I shrugged it off as I made my way to the entrance of John's office. He then gestured to a large cylindrical enclosure that housed several ring-tailed lemurs. Two of the zombie-eyed prosimians let out their high pitched bark-like hoots. John mentioned that those two were the siblings of the lemur that I was here to get. As I followed him into his office I noticed a small rabbit cage that was kept next to his desk. I was astonished with what I saw. A very small lemur was sitting in the corner of the cage rocking back and forth. When John had originally told me that she was blind I was envisioning an animal that would appear to be normal and would merely have a cloudy film over the cornea (like many other blind animals I had met). Upon closer examination, I realized that this little lemur's eyes were far different. In fact she could not even open them due to some strange genetic mutation. John began to tell me the saga of how this little lemur came in from another zoo with her sisters as a yearling. She was placed on exhibit with the other lemurs for several weeks until John arrived one morning and found her lying on the bottom of the enclosure. As he came closer he realized that she was bleeding profusely and that part of her left ear and part of her tail had been torn off. The other lemurs recognized her as a mutant and proceeded to kill her during the night. He immediately rushed her to his veterinarian who stitched her up and placed her on antibiotics. He kept her in the rabbit cage in the office while she recuperated. Now that she had recovered he had no idea what to do with her.

"We can't risk putting her back outside and even if we could, she is just too ugly to put on exhibit. I'll completely understand if you can't take her."

Feeling pure empathy for this poor creature I immediately responded,

"Of course I'll take her."

John then went and quickly pushed her into a small crate and handed it to me. As I made my way back to my van, curiosity got the best of me,

"John, I have to ask, what are all of these noodles in the animal enclosures?"

"Lo Mein noodles, we have a deal with the Chinese restaurant down the street. All of the unused food comes here and we give it to all of the animals. Now that I think about it, your new lemur likes them too."

That was two years ago and "Leona" (as I came to call her) has become a crowd favorite. Teaching children about the importance of tolerance and overcoming adversity. Even though she can't see, she has taken on the look-out role for my main animal building where she lives. Any time she senses something is amiss; an open cage door, an animal missing, or something knocked over, she immediately emits her lemur hoot to tell me that something is wrong. She now carries her friend, a *Curious George* doll, around her enclosure and to every show I do with her. But her most unique trait is her love of Chinese food (Particularly Lo Mein noodles). I am still shocked that anyone could consider this little animal ugly, but in the wise words of Confucius, "Everything has its beauty, but not everyone sees it."

Chapter 23

A Magical Mentor

As I said earlier, Marc Morrone was and still is one of the most influential people in my career. However, there is another "magical" mentor who, over the years, has bent over backwards to help me achieve success. Alan is a fellow animal entertainer/educator who is based in the middle of the country. The big difference: he also operates a sprawling ten acre exotic animal sanctuary on his property where he cares for thousands of animals.

Alan started his business over thirty years ago (before I was even a twinkle in my parent's eyes). He fell into the business as a teenager practicing magic who also happened to have an affinity for animals. One day he was asked to perform a magic show at a children's birthday party and, on the spur of the moment, he decided to bring his pet iguana to the show. History was made. He soon became known as the "Magician who does tricks with exotic animals". His business grew to be one of the most sought after acts in the country by celebrities, schools, and corporate parties. His collection of exotic animals now rivals that of any zoo and his show seamlessly combines the animals with his magical talents.

I first learned of Alan one day when I was watching the evening news. The national news segment was featuring a story of how two men in the country's heartland had been arrested when they brought an illegal pet six foot-long alligator to a local pet store. After the authorities had arrested the men, they called their local animal expert, Alan, to take care of the alligator. The segment went on to show Alan fearlessly grab the alligator and calmly place him in a transport box.

I was impressed, so I immediately ran to my computer so that I could find out more about this amazing man. I then learned of his work rescuing animals and performing amazing animal shows. I had his phone number but developed cold feet and decided not to call him.

Years later, when I started "Animal Adventures" I found his name and phone number and again decided to run a Google search on him. I found that he had since written a book detailing his life and experiences and I promptly ordered it. Upon receipt, I read it cover to cover and was blown away. This was the first time I realized that it is indeed possible to make a living doing animal shows. I then decided to muster up the courage to call Alan using the phone number I had found two years earlier. He picked up and I explained who I was. I explained how inspiring his book had been for me and how I hoped that I could one day follow in his footsteps as a professional animal educator and entertainer. From that point on, Alan took me under his wing and has always shown me the best ways to succeed. He is a treasure trove of information. He's always there for me whenever I have a question about business or an exotic animal. Every few months we call to exchange stories and compare notes. He has even been gracious enough to supply me with some very beautiful and very rare exotic animals that I would otherwise not have been able to get. Alan truly has the magic touch.

Chapter 24

What's Up Doc?

An inconvenient and unfortunate truth in my business is that animals will get sick. When someone has a pet dog or cat they can easily bring it to a local veterinarian who will easily diagnose and treat it. Things are not so straight forward when an exotic wild animal falls ill. Veterinarians typically only receive two days of formal training with exotic animals in their four years of veterinary school. There are many veterinarians who flat out refuse to see exotic animals for this reason alone. On the other side of the spectrum, there are veterinarians who will agree to treat exotic animals, while knowing nothing about them. Even though it can constitute malpractice, there are still disreputable veterinarians who will do it. For many years I was at the mercy of veterinarians at both ends of this spectrum. When one of my beloved exotic animals fell ill, I accepted that they would not recover. That was until one day.

Several years ago I had a small marmoset monkey named "Mowgli". He was about the size of a baseball and was one of my favorite animals. One morning I went to feed him and saw that he was dragging his hind legs behind him as he climbed around his enclosure. I was horrified, mostly because I knew exactly what his problem was: metabolic bone disease. This condition is the equivalent to a person who has rickets. This ailment has plagued captive primates since the beginning of time. Metabolic bone disease occurs when the monkey's body cannot properly absorb calcium, which in turn causes the muscles in the monkey's hind legs to give out and spasm or shake. I immediately rushed him into a local veterinarian who examined him and sent me home with pain medication. That was it.

Several weeks later Mowgli was still not getting better. I decided it was time for a second opinion. As usual, I called Uncle Marc Morrone and explained the predicament to him.

"Why don't you just bring him to Dr. Marder?"

"Who's Dr. Marder?"

Marc went on to explain that Dr. Marder was the best veterinarian he has ever known. In my mind, this meant a lot coming from Uncle Marc. Within the hour I made an appointment to see him.

Upon entry to this veterinary clinic I was met by granite counter tops and a shiny wood floor in the reception area (this was truly one of the nicest veterinary clinics I had ever been in). As I made my way into the exam room I was met by (the one and only) Dr. Marder. I explained Mowgli's problem to him and he genuinely seemed concerned, yet pensive. He immediately weighed Mowgli and pulled out a calculator.

"We need to start him on Calcitonin injections."

I had never heard of this. Dr. Marder went on to explain that Calcitonin is a hormone derived from salmon and was used to treat osteoporosis in women. After three injections, Mowgli began to show signs of improvement. His little hind legs began to regain their strength and his feet began to grasp his branches once again as he climbed throughout his cage: I was sold.

Now whenever one of my animals falls ill, they are immediately rushed to Dr. Marder's clinic. Even though the drive is one hour each way, it is more than worth it, as Dr. Marder has never let me down. No matter what challenge I throw his way (and there have been quite a few) he is always able to cure the offending ailment. Dr. Marder and I have a fantastic working relationship; he even hired me recently to perform at his son's sixth birthday party!

Chapter 25

The Nail Biter

Many years ago, I had a beautiful Scarlet macaw parrot, named Paloma. She was over three feet long and had a gorgeous plumage of yellow, blue, and red. This beautiful bird was given to me by an actor in New Jersey who was moving and could no longer keep her. This species is notorious for being very difficult to handle and she was a challenge from day one. She had a limited vocabulary of "Hi", "Hello", and a sort of "evil" cackle-like laughter that she would usually emit after biting someone. She would happily come out of her cage and perch on my hand and then-*CHOMP*. With her immense beak she would "pinch" the skin on my hand (oftentimes drawing blood) which would always be followed by her "evil cackle". During shows, she would scream bloody murder while waiting her turn in her travel crate. I decided to put up with her eccentricities because she was so beautiful. Don't judge me, any honest man will tell you that there was at least one relationship in their life where they did the same exact thing with a pretty girl!

Several years after I had acquired Paloma I was showing my collection of animals to Maria, my new girl friend at the time. Maria was a medical student who immediately took an interest in my animals due to her background in biology. As we made our way to Paloma's cage she immediately remarked, "What a pretty bird." I warned her not to get too close. I turned my head for a second and immediately heard Paloma's "evil cackle". I quickly turned to Maria who now had both of her hands in her pockets. She promptly responded, "Nothing, I just wanted to see if I could get her to talk." I shrugged off the whole event until a few weeks later when I was watching TV with Maria and noticed that she had a large bandage on her left pinky finger. I immediately began the interrogation.

"What's that bandage for?"

"Do you remember a few weeks back when you were showing me the animals and you heard Paloma laughing? I think I got too close because she grabbed my pinky..."

Maria then proceeded to remove the bandage that was covering her finger. To my horror, half of her pinky nail was completely gone. Paloma had almost severed it.

"Why didn't you tell me this had happened?"

"Well I love the animals just as much as you do and I didn't want to get any of them in trouble."

I soon realized how lucky I was to have a girl friend who was essentially attacked by one of the animals and kept it a secret to protect them. Maria's nail eventually made a full recovery and grew back completely.

Needless to say, the incident was the straw that broke the camel's back. Within a week, Paloma was "banished" to Florida with the kinkajous. Paloma now lives at the Florida sanctuary in a large enclosure near the visitor's entrance, where she delights in tormenting them with her "evil cackle."

Chapter 26

Animal Attacks in the Media

Every few years there always seems to be a horrific attack involving exotic animals and people. Each time this occurs I am often barraged by members of the public who ask me why and how it happened. Let me begin by stating that there is always an inherent risk when one is working with wild animals. No more than driving a car on a busy highway, but it is still a risk. That being said, there are protocols that must be taken when working with wild animals. One of the easiest things that can be done is to prohibit direct contact with any animal that is over fifty pounds. This is why my shows only feature small animals. If you go to many accredited zoos and see training displays featuring elephants or big cats you will see the trainers prompting the animal while they stand behind a chain link fence or a bullet-proof Plexiglas wall. This is to protect the keeper at all times, should the animal decide to attack. Intelligent animal keepers do not anthropomorphize animals. They see them for what they are: wild animals that act purely on instinct. Just because a wild animal is trained, it does not mean it will not attack without cause.

Had Montacore the Bengal tiger, Tillikim the Killer Whale, or Travis the chimp been contained behind a solid barrier, their handlers might have been spared their horrific injuries. These magnificent creatures are still wild at heart and we must always remember that. Unlike humans, wild animals do not need to justify their actions, nor should they. Responsible animal keepers understand this and will do their best to protect both the viewing public as well as themselves from their dangerous charges.

Origins of wild animal attacks can also be traced back to the exotic pet market. Wild animals do not make good pets. I have sacrificed a normal life of vacations, week-end social outings, and children in order to take care of my animals. Few people can make this type of commitment. Wild animals are programmed to be much more active than our domesticated dogs and cats. They are also programmed to be much more aggressive. They have very specific diet needs and require highly specialized veterinary care. Conflicts with humans and wild animals are inevitable when the two share the same living space. Many of the stories you read in the news concerning exotic pets attacking are most often times the result of a truly frustrated animal that was being denied at least one of its basic needs.

Tips for Youngsters

I am always asked by kids how they can be just like me when they grow up. The best piece of advice I can give: don't do what I did! To be where I am today, I received very little formal training in the realm of biology and wildlife management. The only school I went to was the school of "hard knocks" (a term borrowed from Uncle Marc). Most of what I know about animals today was completely self-taught (with the aid of my many mentors). However, I have assembled a few tips for those aspiring veterinarians, animal trainers, biologists, and zoo keepers:

1. *Appreciate* School!

   You hear it all the time from your parents and teachers, but this mindset really will help you. Not only in the animal world, but in any other type of job you may enter as an adult. Every single subject in school teaches us problem solving methods, study techniques, and organizational skills. You will use all three while working with animals!

2. Do well in School!

   Anyone who works with animals had to go to college and get good grades. They had to get good grades while in school to get into college. If you can change your study habits now, then by the time you are in high school getting straight A's will be second nature!

3. Read about animals!

   Be careful of what you read on the internet as it is not always true. Helpful hint: do an "advanced" Google search and search only for websites with ".edu" or ".gov." Anything you can get your hands on that relates to animals, read it!

4. Volunteer! Many colleges require some proof of extracurricular activities and/or community service when they consider your application for admission. Why not utilize your love of animals? Volunteer at an animal shelter, groomery, or even local zoo. You will also learn many interesting things along the way.

5. Major in Biology when you enter college! Even if your college does not offer any courses on zoology or other animal specific fields, fret not! Every doctor, veterinarian, and zoo keeper in the world majored in biology while in college. Once you graduate, you can then market yourself as a biologist and land a job working with animals. Or you may decide to continue on the graduate level and specialize in something more

specific, such as zoology, ornithology, anthropology, etc.

6. Have good luck! A big part of landing a great job working with animals is being in the right place at the right time and being in front of the right person at the right place at the right time. So look for those four-leaf clovers!

7. Find a Mentor!

A mentor is typically a person older than you who teaches and inspires you. Just as I found in Uncle Marc, find an adult who you want to be just like when you grow up. They don't have to be someone working in the animal world. All they need to be is an adult who is willing to teach you and be supportive on your journey towards your dreams. Good candidates for mentors include: parents, grandparents, aunts, uncles, teachers, coaches, and TV personalities (if you're lucky like me!)

Acknowledgements

First, to my friend and mentor, Uncle Marc Morrone, who has always been there for me with his vast knowledge of the natural world. Second, to my wonderful parents, Janice and Glenn, who always encouraged me to follow my dreams. Third, to the love of my life, Maria, you had no idea what you were in for when we first started dating all those years ago! Fourth, to the one and only Doctor Brian Marder, who has performed dozens of miracles before my very eyes. Fifth, to Alan for making my show just as magical as his. Sixth, to *Martha Stewart Living Omnimedia,* for jump starting my TV career. Seventh, to the New York State Department of Environmental Conservation and the United States Department of Agriculture who have always approved my many permit applications which allows me to have a wonderfully fulfilling job.

Biography

"Nature" Nick Jacinto was born in Stony Brook New York and grew up in nearby Setauket. From an early age he knew that he wanted to work with animals. As he got older, he soon realized that he also had a love for performing, teaching, and children. While still in college, he became one of the youngest people in New York to become both a USDA and NYSDEC licensed animal handler, thus allowing him to start his unusual business. He currently owns and operates Animal Adventures, a traveling animal show that seamlessly blends comedy, magic, children, and exotic animals. He and his animals have appeared on numerous TV shows and public events throughout the area. His TV credits include: *The Martha Stewart Show*, *The Wendy Williams Show*, *Petkeeping with Marc Morrone*, *The Today Show*, *Fox & Friends* and *Good Morning America*. He graduated from St.

Joseph's College with BA degrees in General Education, Special Education, and Speech Communications. After graduating he realized that a job as a teacher didn't quite suite him and he started Animal Adventures-he hasn't looked back since!

Visit him online at:

www.AnimalAdventuresParties.com or

www.NatureNick.com

Made in the USA
Middletown, DE
28 March 2015